I0155618

First Light

Poems written by
Beverly George

Copyright © 2022 Beverly George

All rights reserved. No part of this book may be reproduced or transmitted in any form or by any means, electronic storage, and retrieval system, except in the case of brief quotations embodied in critical articles or reviews, without permission in writing from the publisher.

In no way is it legal to reproduce, duplicate, or transmit any part of this document in either electronic means or in printed format. Recording of this publication is strictly prohibited and any storage of this document is not allowed unless with written permission from the publisher.

All rights reserved.

ISBN: 978-1-953760-15-9

Printed in the United States of America

All poems written and copyrighted by Beverly George.

Table of Contents

Foreword

One day I woke up and felt the dawn.

The sun warmed my soul which had been ignored for years of being in survival mode and suddenly I had something to say, write and release into the world.

It was all a mass of colors, and rhythmic ruminations.

I did not know where to begin, how to translate it all.

I had to find the strength, patience, skills, focus, faith, and determination to fashion the colors and sounds into poems that would live and breathe. The results you find here.

In this book, I share works, pieces and poems called "First Light."

I. GRATITUDE

I want to express my thanks and appreciation to God and my parents, Meta Wade George and Albert Lee George, for all they did for me over the years. I am in awe of their devotion and sacrifices made for my education, welfare, and happiness as I grew up in their care. I recognize now how much I benefited from their hard work and dedication.

The word "Thanks" comes from the Latin word "tongere" think. "I will remember what they did for me." I will forever remember and cherish, acknowledge, honor, and celebrate their brave consistency in fighting all manner of circumstances to make my life safe and wholesome, challenging, and honest. I praise their efforts, and accomplishments, commend the noble, spiritual, and practical examples they provided for me and my sister, Margaret Alexandra.

Always responsible, always trustworthy, always dependable, and always loving.

Your humble daughter, forever faithful to your memories,

Beverly

Walk With Me, Lord

■ ■ ■ ■

I put my journey in His Hands and seek to walk with Him, shaping my heart's desires and trusting in His Will. I seek to unlock the treasures in my mind searching for the mind of Christ and His inspiration in all I do. I hope that my actions reflect His Love and concern for my family and friends, for those in my path each day. I seek confirmation that my deeds are aligned with His Word and I study it diligently with purpose for deep understanding and insight.

I stumble yet know He will forgive, catch me and lift me up through His Grace and Mercy. I know that my steps will be guided and directed if I ask Him to walk with me. His Word is a constant light unto my path.

He is my fortress and my stronghold, always before me and with me. He surrounds me with His Love and Kindness. Never will I want for necessities for He is my Provider and Protector in times of trouble. He is my King and Sovereign Lord. He is my Everlasting Father.

He is able to do all things. In His Name, I pray and give Him all the Glory!

Amen.

Myrteen W. King

■ ■ ■ ■

Flown to the other side of the mirror,

Spirited through the image to the

Essence inside the vision,

Connecting her soul to God.

Rendering her to stars, and moons of yesteryear and
tomorrow.

Halting the beating of her heart forevermore to

Yield to the calling of Hereafter,

Beyond where we speak in tongues

unknown to mortals.

The reflecting glass looks back at us one day

letting us through to the other side.

We too, will jump this final broom

from the dust, as Myrteen, and

consummate our destiny.

He is Always with Us
■ ■ ■ ■

He is always with us like air is always in us,
love that never leaves us.
First kiss that keeps reminding us of
a promised day.

He is always with us,
a strong branch you can cling to
even if friends leave you
and cannot be found.

Closer than why in you and yes in me.
Closer than rain in drops
as they kiss the sea.
Closer than blue in the Blues, red in all our blood.
He is always with us,
Every single minute
With us,
you and me.

Your Glory (A Prayer)

■ ■ ■

Increase my understanding of your Glory.

Enlarge my capacity.

Expand my horizons.

Elevate my character.

Deepen my qualities.

Soften my heart.

Open my inner eye.

Infuse me with your spirit of loving-kindness.

Let me drink from your Words

As a plant from underground springs.

They are like your hidden wisdom flowing in secret places

in my heart.

Quiet, yet pronounced,

with fierce beauty,

outstretched, radiant,

red blossoms unfurl above.

Abundant joy.

Accept, receive, attain.

I see and know,

Your Glory.

The Open Door
■ ■ ■ ■

When I open the door of the church
God holds me in the music, in the prayers,
in the scriptures, in the sacred moments.
I join souls communing with Him.
We reverence His Honor, Majesty, Power, and Command.

When I open the door to the church
I open my being, and call out to my Creator Who asks the
best of me to come forth and be touched by Him.
That He will bless me with His Infinite Love and Wisdom,
that He will bestow upon me a better understanding of His
Words, how to interpret them,
how I should relate to my fellow human beings,
how I should walk, talk, and think every day.
What I should do and say and how I should be or not be.

When I open the door of the church, I step into a different
atmosphere.
Worldly cares do not tug at my hem.

or clutter my mind with noise.
Sweet spirituals surround me
carrying me to a realm of happiness and joy
where the souls of my ancestors abide.
A fount of life-giving waters refresh my weary, beaten soul
and I find the strength to fight the battles of this life.

When I open the door of the church, His love floods my
soul and rushes toward me like the Light of a new day, full
of promise.
Rounded ceilings, like a womb embraces those within its
all-encompassing,
Protection,
A cocoon from which we will one day emerge as angels at
His feet.

I open the door. I am there as I am here.
I am His,
Yet with my church family.
Each in individual
circumstances worshipping our
Jesus who died on the Cross,
and rose on the third day.

When we open the door of the church

the power of His Precious Blood.

washes our souls,

and we are transformed.

The Sea

■ ■ ■ ■

The sea moves ships to distant lands,
Inspires us to understand,
Whenever we have been knocked down,
Prayers for success
Must be found
To spur us with promise anew
And goals once more we must pursue.

Tides out and in,
Like a refrain,
Balance
Our love
As He sustains

The lullaby, its calming sound,
Above gulls soaring, heaven bound.
The sea in all our hearts instills,
Currents of
His Almighty Will.

II. Land of the Free

No more jumping rope in the backyard in Mt. Vernon,

dreaming of when I could stay up past 7:30

and drive a car.

My mother, born in South Carolina, was hoping

vicious dogs would not snarl at my heels.

My father, who returned from the Army, was hoping the
final flames of WWII would not

scorch my youth.

But newspapers reported the

bombing of Black churches.

The devil had designed new clothes,

To terrorize with white bedsheets on horseback,

To restrict Blacks with legislation,

gerrymander and voter suppression.

We lived in the

We lived in a land where Blacks were enslaved,

instead of the "Land of the free and the home of the brave."

My parents did not describe lynching then
as I jumped rope long ago.
Reality closed in like a thick curtain.
All whites were not great. They were not all full of hope.

Brutal facts of Tulsa, Wounded Knee and more,
tried to crush the spirit.
My schoolbooks failed to teach
Africa's glory, Virginia's trade, Douglas's oratory.
All missing from classes in history.

Not in the backyard in Mt. Vernon anymore.
Bare depression now where I had jumped rope.
Couldn't find the land for which our fathers fought
Where great, great, grandfathers had been bought.

The jump rope disappears in the rearview mirror.
I read signs as I drive through shifting terrain
To the coveted
"Land of the free,
and the home of the brave".

We are the Other

■ ■ ■ ■

1700.

Ships bellies burst

Black cargo, gold.

Nostrils filled,

Stench foul,

Human beings, sold.

We are the other, in the land of another.

Replaced African names with "Toby" and "Tom"

Plantations destroyed family bonds.

Children torn.

Screaming from their mother's arms.

We are the other, in the land of another.

The slave's bible,

Omitted key texts,

"Let my people go" from Exodus,

To keep us from fleeing

The whip and the beatings.

We are the other, in the land of another.

2022

Some took issue with
"Learning while Black" at
HBCUs
Neo Nazis threatened Black schools with bombs.
The nation was frightened and alarmed.
We are the other, in the land of another.

After King and Obama's day,
We persevered, a new way.
We will banish all fears and
More than fulfill,
Dreams of the slaves
We protected for years.

We fight for the land where we are all brothers,
Study Black history with all the others,
Vote for our candidates. Do what is right.
Say our names loud, hold our children tight,

Let the next generation finally see
Brothers built this land,
Home of the free.

No Fool

■ ■ ■ ■

Mama didn't raise no fool.

Didn't spend time in your slanted schools

to be tucked in a self-righteous pocket in tears

where you thought I'd be

stuck for the rest of my years.

I'm not biding my time or biting my tongue.

If you think I'm bad, I have just now begun.

In wars almost died, and at home called a nigger.

Bullets from cops. White finger on the trigger.

Boy with skittles shot in the street.

Wrong apartment, and no knock decree.

If more cops on tasers would first rely,

fewer unarmed Black men would have had to die.

Lawyers appear too late for the deceased.

We cannot bring George Floyd back to his feet.

From graveyards, Black lives cannot be appealed.

In the end, only painful morals revealed.

We need to live by that Golden Rule
that was taught so diligently in your schools.
We are each of us God's child to defend.
What we do will come back to us all in the end.
Mama didn't raise no fool!

Who Do You See

■ ■ ■ ■

Black kin of some someone
from Africa's shores,
Once packed in a ship
brought o'er vast ocean floors.

Working fields
from dawn to dusk,
slaves choked with fear
turned into dry husks.

Do you see through
blue eyes so fair,
Black girls in church
bombed for worshipping there?

Shameful deeds marring the past,
cry out for freedom's promise.
Judicious mandates we must cast
and build on love inside us.

I am descended from royal blood,
born near the ancient Nile,
cradle of civilization, a word
you often interpret with guile.

I am a rock on the shore of life,
seen storms unleashed by the devil,
stood up to evil, horror, and strife,
come back from deep heartache to revel.

In the love of the Lord, Who eases all pain.
My poor humble life He sustained.
When all else is gone,
we are not ours alone.

Who do you see when you look at me?
Tell me, who do you see?

History

■ ■ ■ ■

This question is burning in me.
Where is our true history?
Intelligence mocks the white version
for we would deny their revision.

What do you endorse or subscribe
to support, adhere to, advise?
Unmarked Black graves are now lost
'neath lynching trees bent in remorse.

Killed in Tulsa and Wounded Knee,
Middle Passage now under the sea?
Where are those lost people like me?
and what about their legacies?

Where can we stand
in our tortured land
if we can't find
our history?

Let us never again run down
those winding dark paths underground.
Duplicitous secrets they needed
in the perilous past now defeated.
The establishment surely will fall
when unbiased facts are now recalled.

I must continue this task.
Search for the whole story at last.
The inclusive all too human mysteries
will be found in the unabridged history.

Whisper in the Winds

■ ■ ■ ■

Ocean waves wash the shore only to recede,

driving closer over smooth sand to touch,

your skin feeling the cool water and the sun warms your
face.

Beauty intoxicates.

Timeless awareness

overrides the senses.

Mysteries commune.

As you stand

under that blue sky, deep in crystal water,

Spirits of our honored ancestors

Whisper in the winds.

Ancestors

■ ■ ■ ■

Spirits of the ancestors

within us,

protect and strengthen,

breathe wisdom of ages

before

we were born.

Unfettered, unencumbered,

defining,

completing and,

guiding us,

with love.

Suffering souls found somber solace,

fierce bonds,

soothing balm.

No one was alone. All aligned.

Those once enslaved sustaining hope each in the other,

brother, sister, mother, father, friend, cousin,

Abide with,

the spirits of the

Mighty ancestors.

Persistent Rivals

■ ■ ■ ■

Toni Morrison and Angela Davis,
writers in a photo
walking down N.Y. Street
side by side, afro halos crowning,
share what only genius know.

Their work explains justice again and again
but those
still clinging to remnants of wrong
continue to stitch clothes with sin.
Cloth dyed in indelible blues,
Stiff collar stays,
Proper ties around necks,
Frustration, chokes,
Threatens eyes
look the other way.

We still see
Truth has persistent rivals.

III. Poems From Her Soul

She sits and writes
poems from her soul.
She cannot sing.
Her breath will not carry her voice anymore.
She cannot play.
Her fingers will not manipulate
the keys of black and white,
laid out in twos and threes
and so she writes these verses.

First to win a place in her universe,
in this world of letters
invisibly touching
ours, yours, and mine.

An architect, bravely penetrating meanings,
skipping through syntax, researching derivations,
dissecting down to their syllabic toes,

origins, innuendoes, strengths and shadows.

She loves, plays with, manipulates, positioning them as on a chess board,

as if her heartbeats depended on their rhythms.

She loves them passionately,

They are a consolation,

myriad variations.

She writes poems from her soul...

Poems

■ ■ ■ ■

Poems are within me.

not out there,

flying like butterflies to be

captured in a net,

but rather, they call to be released from the world

inside my heart.

Words play, phrases trip the tip of the tongue.

Memories compete for

a path,

for recognition, understanding,

They don't care if the sun is up,

I am dressed or my teeth are brushed.

Build a new and

Navigate the Stars.

First Word

■ ■ ■ ■

Out of bed.

Reign in your dreams.

Clock is urging you begin.

Step into the verdant forest

where others have played this part,

where you walk your path alone,

where you write for rainy hours.

where you draw strength from your soul,

where first word searches for others,

hidden meanings to unfold,

then you find an oval clearing,

ending the winding dirt road.

Rainbow shimmers

up ahead.

Words reflecting love and sorrows,

victory, tears, and tomorrows

form at last before your eyes,
captured moments from the journey
in the notebook at your side
your poems are carefully written
like pink roses pressed in time.

War

■ ■ ■ ■

Insanity rattles its ancient saber.
Slays civil thoughts.

Lives destroyed.
No one is saved.
Ruined lives
Orders obeyed.

When greed defies reason
Evil takes the throne.
Burns body and heart,
Mocks silver and gold.

Death dressed as War,
Preys
Again.

Love Thy Neighbor

■ ■ ■ ■

Love thy neighbor as thyself.

Step one, love yourself.

It does not mean

Sate your ego with things,

Keep up with the Jones'

With a new Mercedes,

Bask in the limelight by throwing shade,

Get over on friends cause you've got it made.

We are blocked from loving ourselves

Because we know

The legacy of slavery

masks what we show.

How we treated slaves in our mass memory,

An inscrutable wall between you and me.

Disproportionate Blacks in prison and, poor,

Inadequate health care, housing and more.

How can we right, centuries gone awry,

Decades of duplicitous deceit and lies?

Admit, don't deny sins too heinous to utter,
 Inhumanity of what was done for a dollar,
By misguided deviants, before we were born,
Whose history of dark deeds will never be shorn.

Coursing through our veins residue of its poison.
God, purify the blood of this generation.

Behold God in the eyes of thy neighbor's face.
Therein self-love starts, therein lies His Grace.
These are who we are charged to embrace.
The burning bush our hearts will replace.

Honor, reveal, and build on the past.
We can grasp,
"Love thy neighbor."
At last.

School Shootings

∎∎∎∎

19 children and two teachers met violent deaths
in Uvalde's school shooting,
May 2022.

 Rather not see
report of bright
blue and orange
superhero coffin for
a six-year-old body.
I wish the boy was
Alive,
safe in his innocence
instead of his grave.

The nation's grief falls, like night.
fatal rerun left us stunned and dismayed.
been here before, regrets haunting our pain.
eyes bloodshot and red, opens that familiar wound,
 owed to ignored posts and unchecked weapons.

Prayers offered, again,
congress debates again,
will children in its wake
learn to trust again?

Defies and denies
logic and life.
"Must not happen again",
is that hope merely
futile exercise
as we count lifeless bodies
strewn before our eyes?

Now on the map,
tragedy claims,
Uvalde, Texas
immortal stain.

Numbers

Oh, the numbers they count when we're in the womb,
then the date our life on this earth we assume.
Oh, the numbers we learn on our fingers and toes,
and she will make music wherever she goes.

The number of sheep we count in our beds,
and sugar plum fairies dance in our heads.
Oh, the numbers that catalog Bible verses,
keeping us righteous so God can find us.

The number of the hard-earned salary we pay
for our mortgage, utilities, and food for the day.
Oh, the number of times we wish we had time
to turn back the clock and start over the climb.

Oh, the number we pledged to our alma mater

which gave us the means to live how we want to.
Oh, the number of children we pray someday
will care for us when our strength fades away.

Oh, the number of cell phones you have on one plan,
one for the office and one for the fam.
Oh, the secret social security one,
that you promise not to reveal or divulge.

Oh, the number of channels on cable TV
for here and back to uncertainty.
Oh, number the candles on birthday cakes
symbolize victory and lonely heartache.

Oh, number the body count now in Ukraine.
the world prays for peace. War we cannot sustain.
Number the years of love, death, and mirth
until we sleep finally under the earth.

Again

■■■■

Raucous laughter
bounced off the walls,
rolled down the floors of the
empty high school hall,
threatening to
topple him like an
unsteady
bowling pin.

He felt them creeping up behind.
He fell.
Those four laughed even louder,
'till they had their fill of the echoes off the waxed tiles.
They left him alone on the floor in a heap.

He pulled up, knelt, and regained his footing.
Found his glasses, zipped his torn jacket, and put on his
stained cap.
Escaped under the red exit letters

into the chilly wind.

Alone, defeated, shaken,

Again.

Wild Roses

■■■■

Wild roses bloom rampant.
Wrapped around a white picket fence
Facing the rambling road.
Their beauty renders me silent.

Footsteps fall down the back steps.
The porch door slams behind you.
Your silhouette with suitcase swinging moves quickly to the
car.
"Come back!" I shout.
"Take me with you."
The words blow into the wind.
My thoughts run away with me paralyzed there in the yard.
How will I live without you?
A stream of tears flows down my face.
I shrink inside the house to the sound of the engine.

Faint scent of wild roses followed me in.
Sun has since set.
Road took you miles beyond the fence.
Heartache emboldened the silence.

Life

■ ■ ■ ■

Life is not judged in hours or minutes,
but in laughter, sunsets, and morning dew,
mountains, rainbows, and carousels,
first kisses, tears, dancing, and drums,
toddler's steps, coming home smiles and hugs.

rosebuds, Christmas, marching bands,
spirituals, symphonies, bedtime prayers,
snowflakes, spring showers, shooting stars,
summer evenings in the park
holding your hand in the dark…
The ordinary and sublime
cannot be measured solely
In time.

Star

■■■■

A star in each of us every day
which we must find
in our own way.
A divine light in
our heart to share
before we pass away.

It brightly glows
no one need compare
the gifts and talents
In our care.

We light the skies
across the world
each man, woman
boy and girl.

We thwart what evil-doers could
with strategies and plans for good.

We sing the praises of His Glory
with joyous hymns and heroic stories.

This little poem started from
the truth of one small star far-flung.
The universe surrounding asks,
"What will your star become at last?"

The Closet

■ ■ ■ ■

My shoes are in shock,

fearing my ten extra pounds.

Old handbags in the corner secret pennies to be found.

Worn sweaters, shiver lonely without a sound.

Dried corsage sighs from the shelf above...

Mugs for regifting pray for a home.

Hanging red scarf,

Anxious for winter's cue.

I shut the door keeping all from view.

Dandelions

■ ■ ■ ■

June 7, 2022

At first dandelions
don't boast beauty.
weeds after all.

Musty odor,
Leaves dull, hint of gray,
still they stand proud.

Yellow flowers become white puffs
like ballerinas cling,

A child's wish launches.
dancers pirouette in the breeze.

Dark Angel

∎ ∎ ∎ ∎

June 22, 2022

Age looks at me
in the mirror tonight.

Lipstick fond, fierce defense.
Foundation lies
thick on thinning skin,
Concealing
sinner within.

"How much more time on stage?"
I try to gauge,
they insist curtain calls,
bows from the waist,
adieu to the clamoring crowd.

Dark angel alights
in the wings.

Circus

■ ■ ■

My father took correspondence courses in the fifties
to pursue his passion for writing.
after long days of working at the post office
 I could hear
through my bedroom door, him typing
late into the night.

One particular day in spring, he decided to meet
with my fifth-grade English teacher
 who had harshly criticized my poetry.
This is the only time his person
entered the brick schoolhouse door.

She, in a gray knit suit with pearls swinging,
wispy bleached blond strands framing
 her nervous face with red lips smiling,
stiffly lowered into the chair,
the wooden desk in front of the blackboard.
he carefully in the designated seat beside her
hat in hand.

Formalities attended; they reviewed my poem "Circus" –
maybe she didn't understand why
 I purposely used that word to describe
the world parading in front of my ten-year-old eyes.

"It depends on your perspective, Miss Wilkins,"
 he said, laying his brown hands on the desk.
She slid her glasses down her nose,
silent implication awaiting its due.
"I guess she has expressed a particular point of view."
Rethinking the grade
reluctant respect hovered like her bright red pen writing on
the page.
Miss Wilkins gave my poem an A instead of a C.
after showing alliteration in verses one and three.

My father passed on
his dream of writing to me.
Having to support the family,
took a second job in upholstery.
Hammered nails, building sofas at night till late,
while I donned the mantel he wanted to take.

His hands on the desk, what Miss Wilkins found,

could raise the grade for all in our circus crowd.

Acknowledgments

Like you, I have loved books and reading for years. Only recently did I think I would embark upon writing one of my own. It has been years in the making but all good things take time. Most of my life has been devoted to musical pursuits as I was born with some talent that my parents encouraged and I was able to develop through the years but hidden away was a hope to write which I never abandoned. My retirement has given the opportunity to fan this flame.

My parents instilled in me a love of literature, poetry, the Bible, and history for which I am deeply grateful. I draw on them daily as they add a rich dimension to my life and work. Poets such as Phyliss Wheatley, Paul Lawrence Dunbar, Langston Hughes, and Maya Angelou have been inspirations, as well as Gwendolyn Brooks, Joy Harjo, Billy Collins, Amanda Gorman and others have been major influences.

I was raised in Mt. Vernon, N.Y., and graduated from Smith College in 1973. I married and had three wonderful children, divorced in 1980, and moved to South Carolina in '98 to care for ailing parents who passed away in 1998 and 2000. I remained in South Carolina and taught music for 22 years in public schools, earned two master's degrees in Education and National Board Certification in Elementary Choral Music.

I thank my former husband, Douglas F. Ruhe, children Jamal (Alice Quinn), Shamsi and Husayn Ruhe, grandsons, Jason, William and Malcolm Ruhe, sister M. Alexandra George of Minneapolis, college friend Lee Howell of Florida, Cousin Charlotte Moore of N.Y., Cousin Debbie Singletary of S.C., cousin James Williams of WA, Aunt Annie Mae Wade Williams, Aunt Mary Wade Moore and Aunt Florence Rebecca Wade Bush.

I am a member of Mt. Pisgah Missionary Baptist Church in Rembert, S.C., several writing groups, book clubs, and alumnae associations.

Thank you also to Dr. Marita Kinney, CEO and Publisher of Pure Thoughts Publishing for her patience and expertise.

This selection of original poems as a first work would not have been possible without those named above. My deep thanks to them and to the Almighty Father who orchestrates my life.

Beverly George

Beverly George was raised in Mt. Vernon, N.Y. and graduated from Smith College in 1973. She married Douglas Ruhe and has three wonderful children, Jamal, Shamsi and Husayn. After 19 years she divorced and moved to South Carolina in '98 to care for her parents, Meta and Albert George, who passed away in 1998 and 2000. While in South Carolina teaching music for 22 years in the public schools, she earned two master's degrees in Education and National

Board Certification in Elementary Choral Music. She joined Mt. Pisgah Missionary Baptist Church in Rembert, S.C. in 1999 and Wesmark Book Club in Sumter in 2020 as well as other online book clubs and alumnae associations. She travels to upstate N.Y. and New Orleans to visit children and grandchildren, Jason, William and Malcolm. She has family gatherings at the home her parents left to her and her sister, Margaret. Upon retirement in 2020 she began online classes with Curtis Brown Creative, Writers.com, Brooklynpoets.org, and plans to pursue a low residency MFA in poetry in January.

www.ingramcontent.com/pod-product-compliance
Lightning Source LLC
La Vergne TN
LVHW051817080426
835513LV00017B/1996